PŘÍBĚH ČÍSEL

THE NUMBER STORY

SMALL BOOK ONE

ENGLISH - CZECH

*Numbers Teach Children
Their Number Names*

written and illustrated by

MISS ANNA

Early Reader Edition of *The Number Story 1*
Bronze Medal Winner, 2016 Wishing Shelf Book Award

Cover by | Lumpy Publishing
Layout by | Lumpy Publishing
Translated by Dita
Coloring by Jieeun Woo and Maria Mirabella

Library of Congress Control Number: 2018902040

Names: Miss Anna, author.
Title: Number story : numbers teach children their number names / Miss Anna.
Description: Portland, OR: Lumpy Publishing, 2018.
Identifiers: ISBN 978-1-945977-37-4| LCCN 2018902040
Summary: The pictures and rhymes present stories which introduce numbers 0-10.
Subjects: LCSH Numeration—English--Czech--Pictorial works--Juvenile literature. | BISAC JUVENILE NONFICTION /
Languages: English--Czech
Classification: LCC QA141.3 .M57 2018 | DDC 513—dc23

Publisher: Lumpy Publishing
Website: www.missannabooks.com
Email: missanna@missannabooks.com

Paperback: ISBN 978-1-945977-37-4
Printed in the U.S.A.   1 3 5 7 9 10 8 6 4 2

Chceš znát jména čísel?

It is very easy and a lot of fun!

Je to velice jednoduché a zábavné.

Say-along our little jingle

Opakuj s námi tento krátký příběh!

starting from Number One!

Začneme tedy jedničkou!

1

ONE   looks like my one finger.

JEDNIČKA

vypadá jako můj prstík.

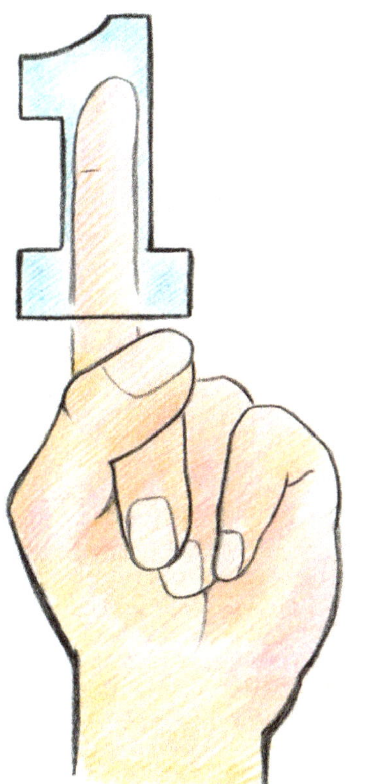
ONE!
JEDNA!

2
TWO   trails a tail.
DVA
na mě vrtí ocáskem.

A TAIL! OCÁSEK!

THREE has bumps.

TROJKA

mi připomíná kopečky.

Podívej se na ty kopce!

4

FOUR carries a sail.

ČTYŘKA

je vlnící se plachetnice.

4
A SAIL!
PLACHETNICE!

5

FIVE is a racing track.

PĚT

je dráha pro závodní autíčka.

VROOM
UŽ JEDOU!

SIX   curves like a snail.

ŠEST

se plazí jako sneček.

A SNAIL! ŠEČKU!

7

SEVEN has a sharp angle.

SEDM

je ostrá jako hrana.

BE CAREFUL! IT'S SHARP!

Pozor! Je to ostré!

8

EIGHT   is rollercoaster rails.

OSM

to je horská dráha.

JUPÍÍÍ!
YIPPEE!

NINE is a bubble on a stick.

DEVĚT

je bublina na tyčce.

A BUBBLE! BUBLINA!

TEN   is an eye of a whale.

DESÍTKA

je velrybí očko.

MRK MRK!
WINK!
HELLO! AHOJ!

And A
0
ZERO is an empty pail.
NULA
je prázdný kbelík.

IT'S
EMPTY!
Je prázdný!

Thank you for playing with us today.

We had a lot of fun too!

Děkujeme že sis s námi dneska zahrál!

Užili jsme si spoutu zábavy!

We are your Number friends,
Zero to Ten,
Who will be here for you~

Jsme tví číselní kamarádi
Jedna až Deset.
Vždycky s tebou budeme!

Bye-bye now!
See you again soon!

Tak ahoj!
Brzy se uvidíme!

The Numbers are *SINGING* too!

To sing-a-long, look for Miss Anna Number Story
at your favorite music store like iTUNES.

MP3

Numbers 0-10
IDENTIFYING
& COUNTING

Number Story 1 & 2

isbn: 978-0-996216-48-7

Numbers 11-20
& Ordinals

first, second, third...

Number Story 3 & 4

isbn: 978-1-945977-01-5

Numbers 0-100
& Place Values

ones, tens, hundreds...

Number Story 5 & 6

isbn: 978-1-945977-06-0

About Clocks
& Telling Time

hours, minutes, seconds

Number Story 7 & 8

isbn: 978-1-949320-40-4

For more Miss Anna books to love,
visit us at

www.missannabooks.com

Numbers are working hard all over the world!
Come Travel the World with Us!

Milton Keynes UK
Ingram Content Group UK Ltd.
UKHW021547260324
439986UK00005B/56